The Book Be Long to

....

Cactus

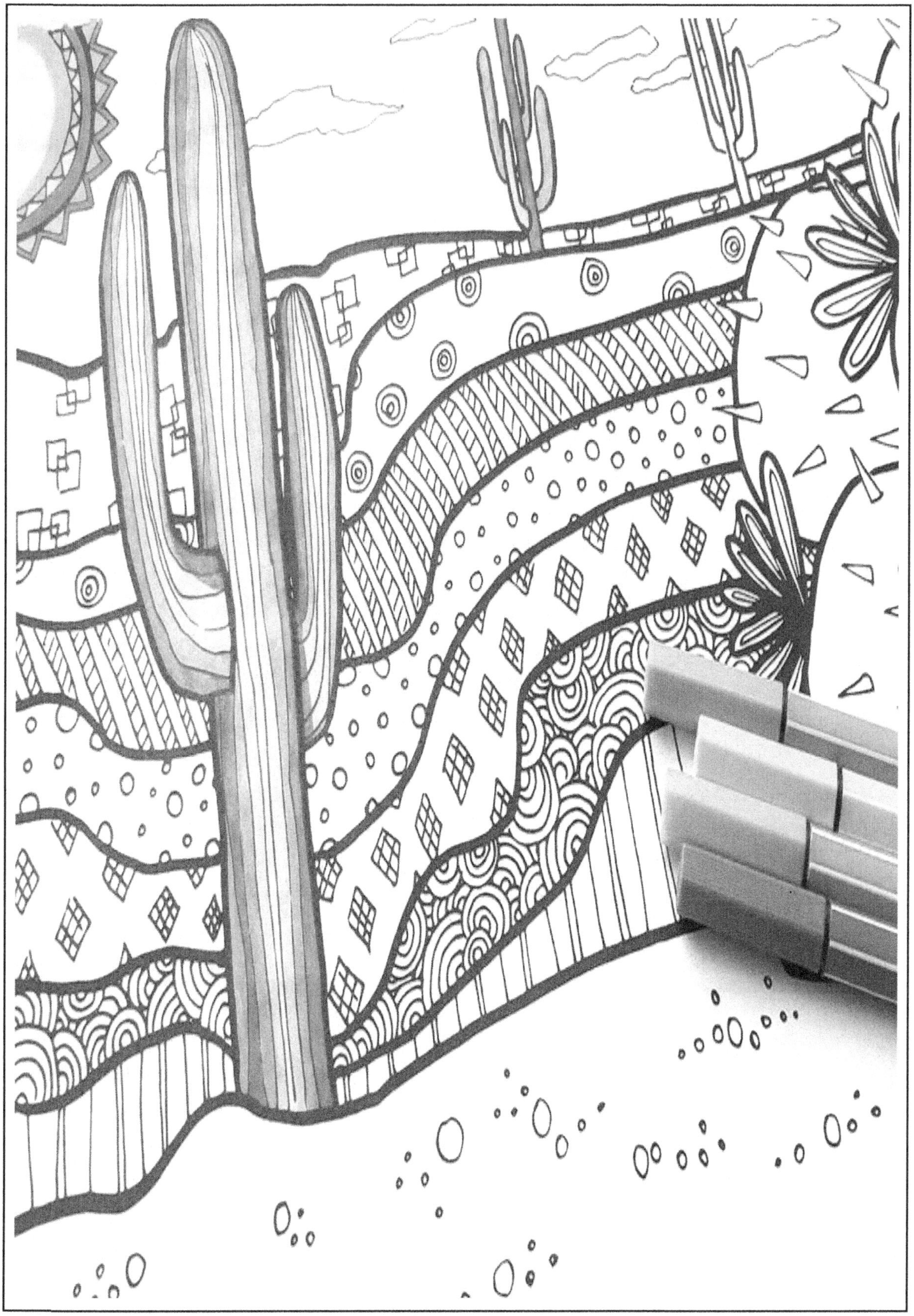

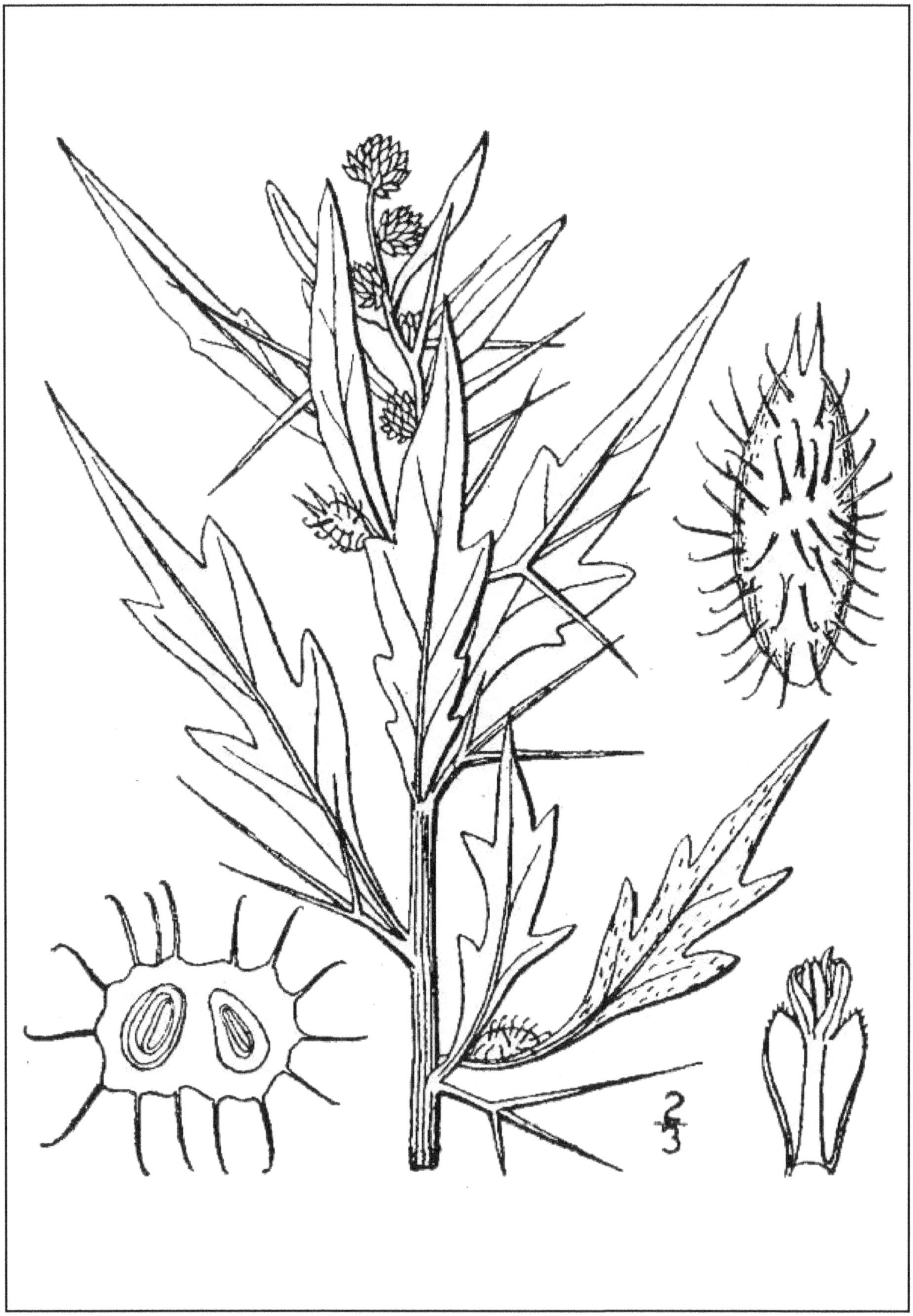
2/3

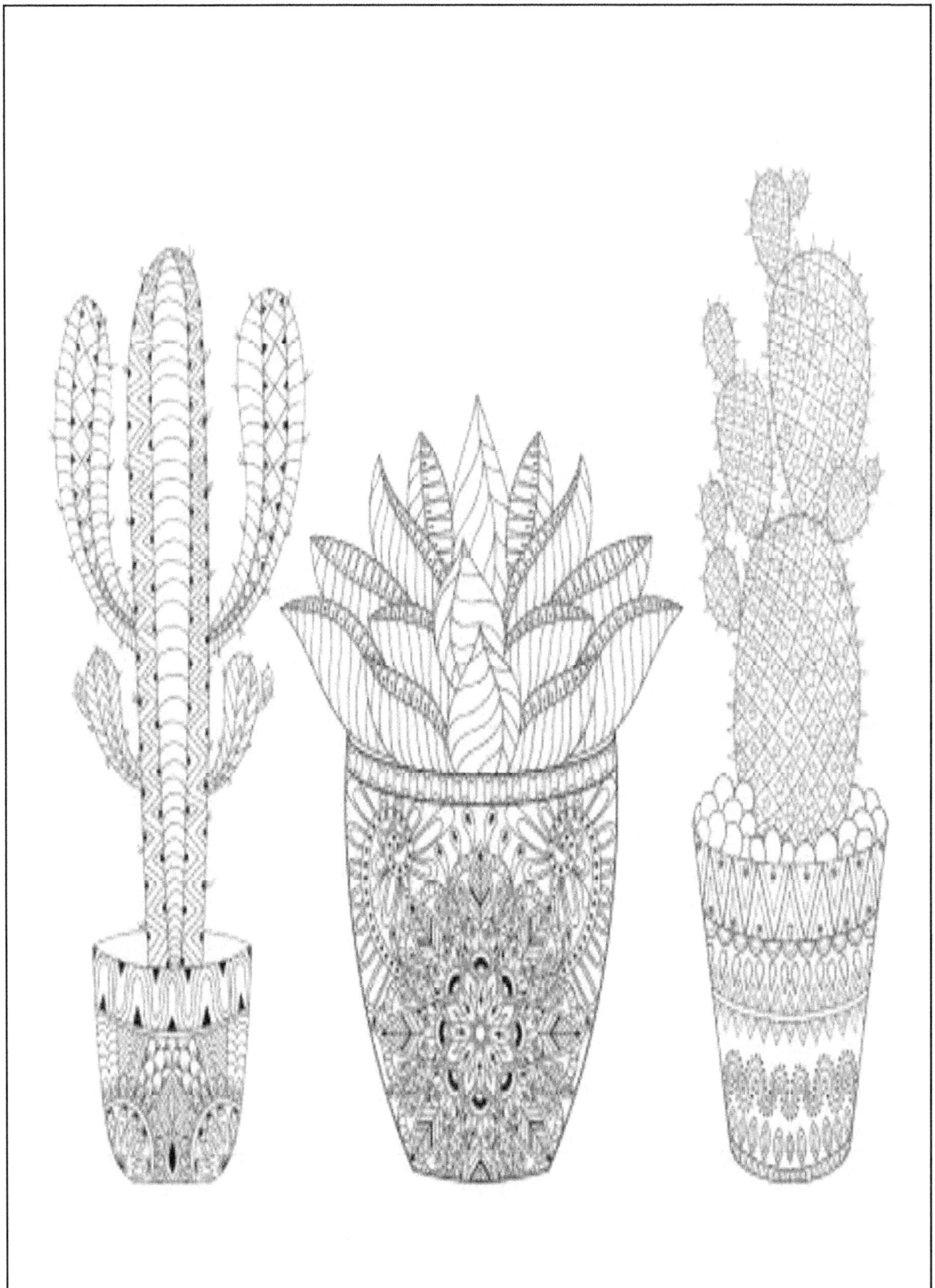

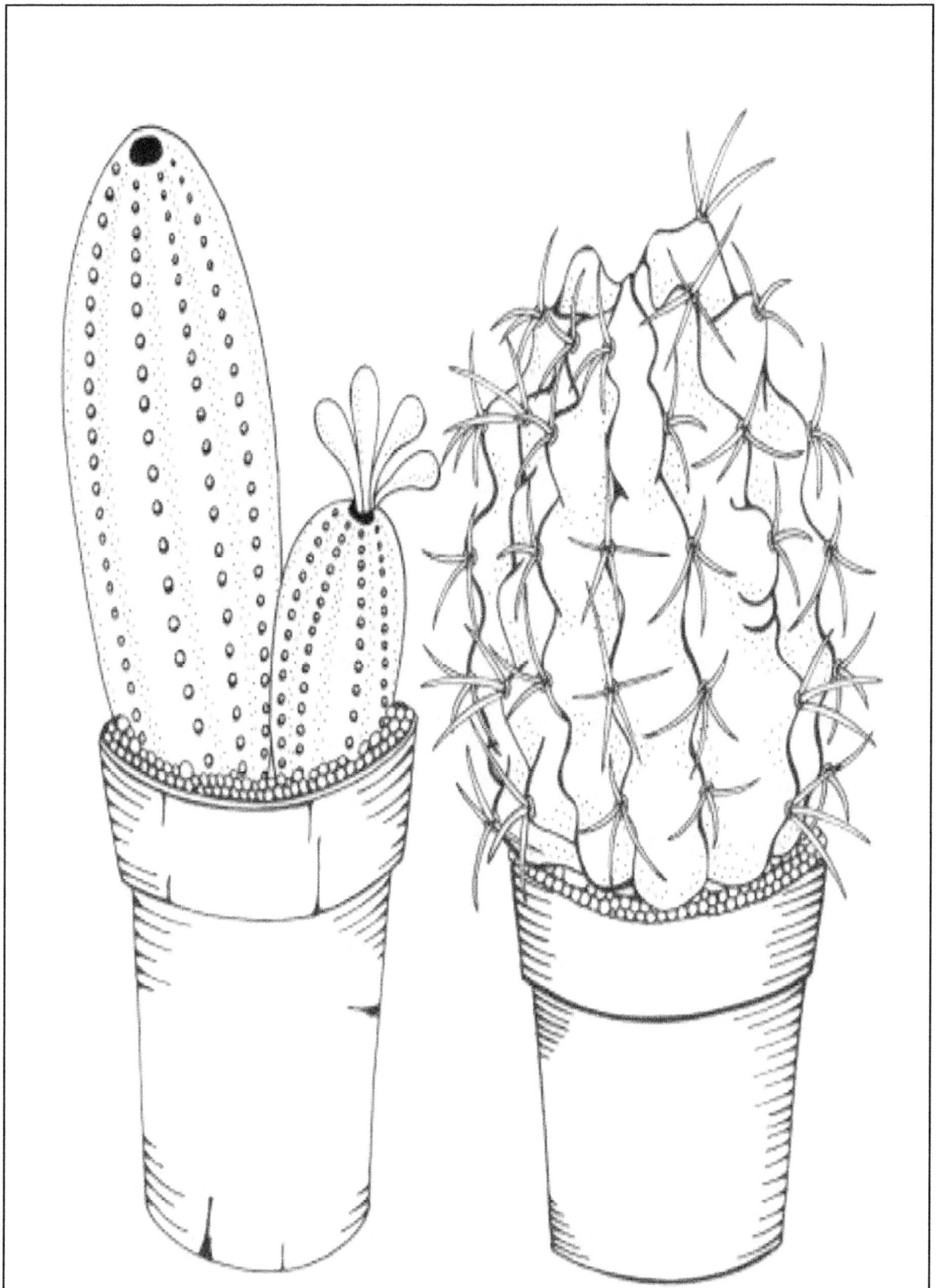

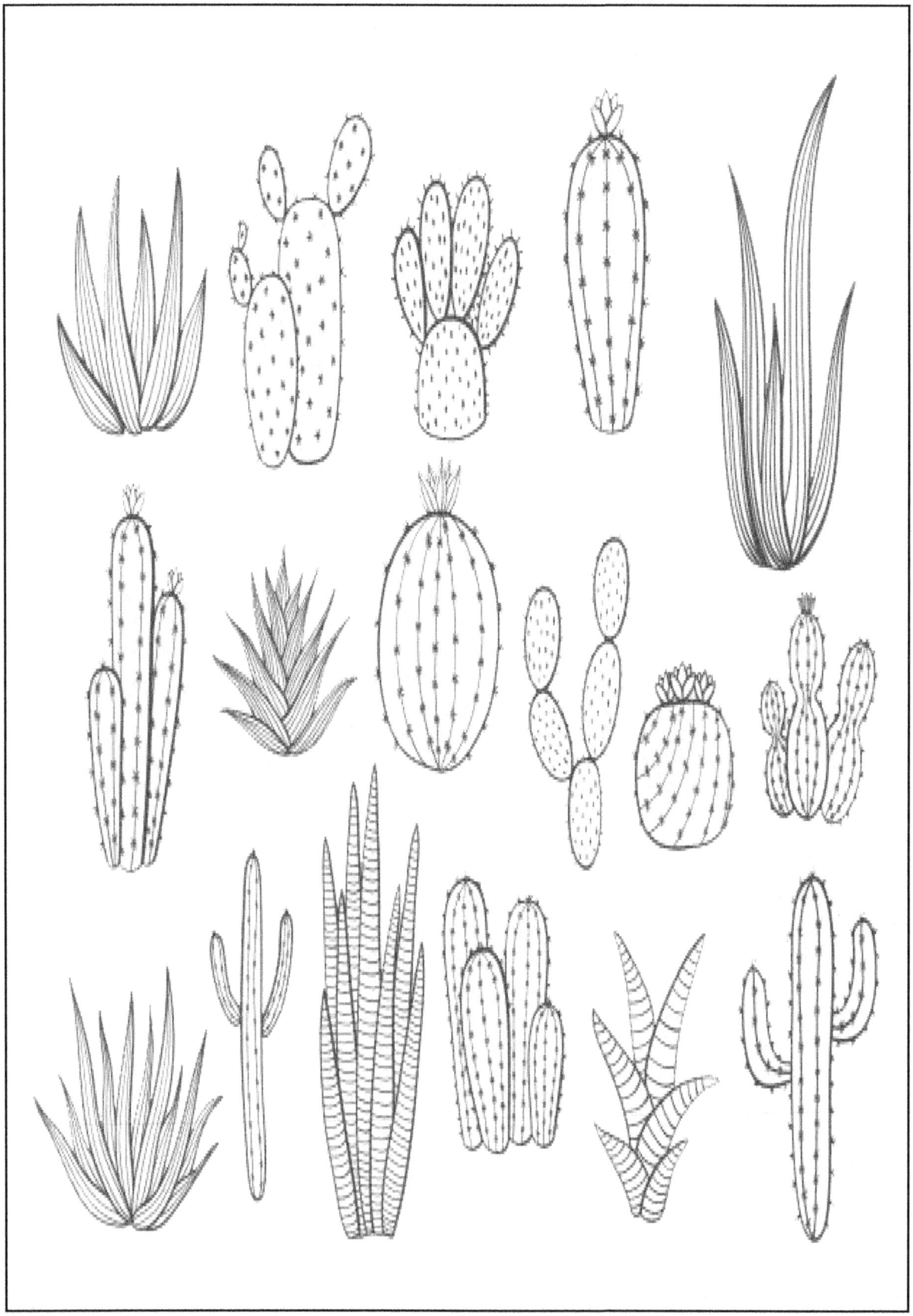

95

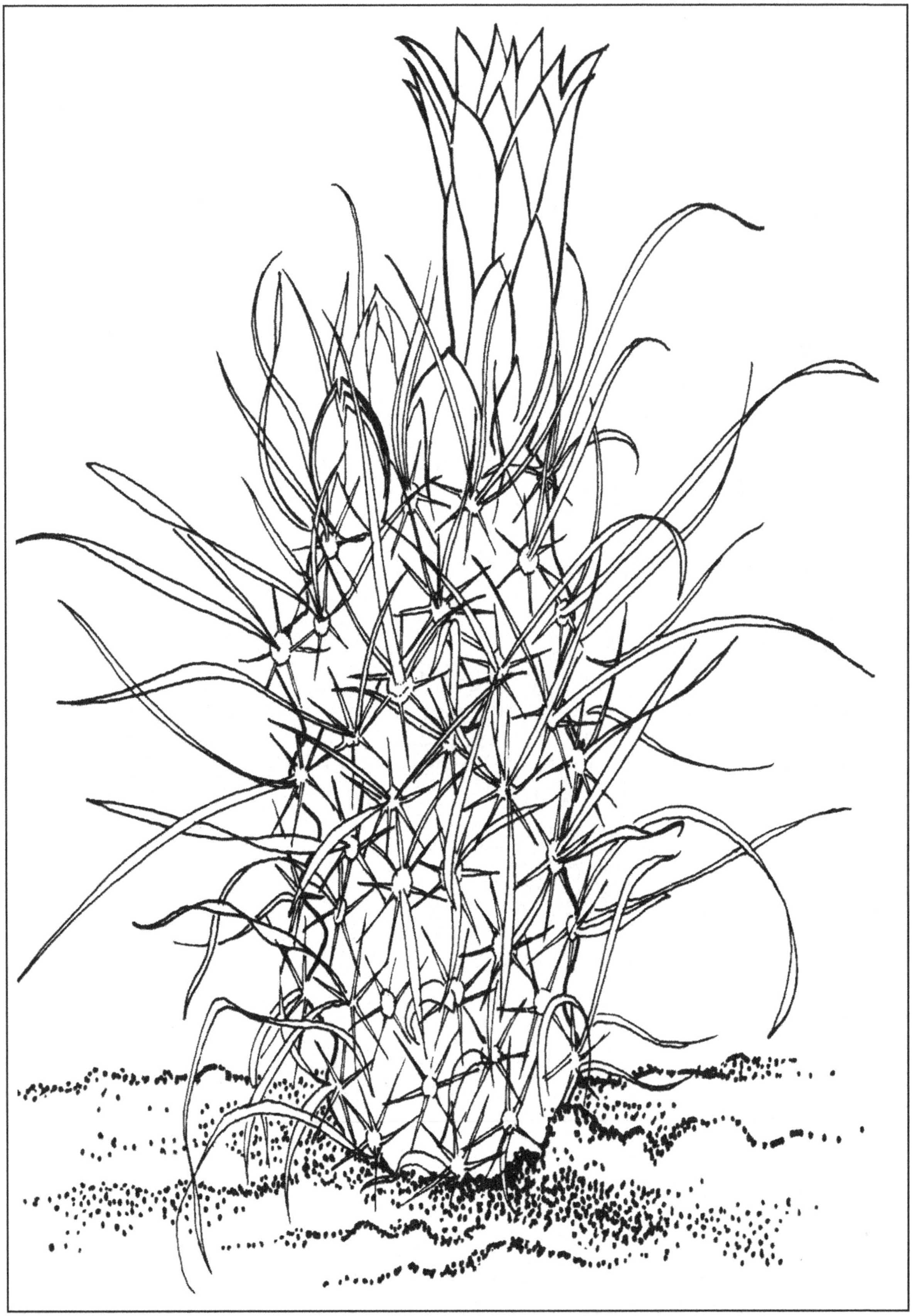

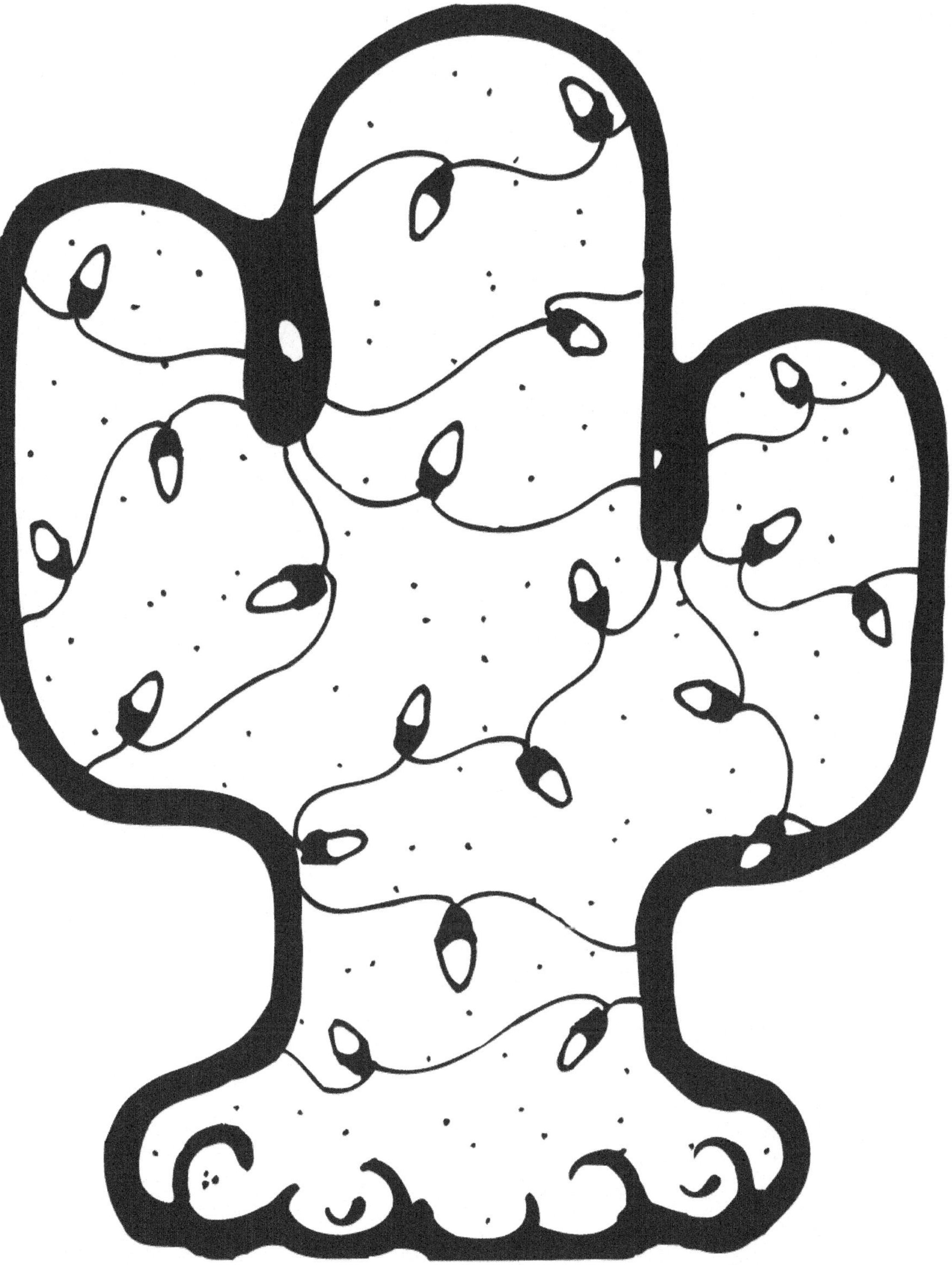

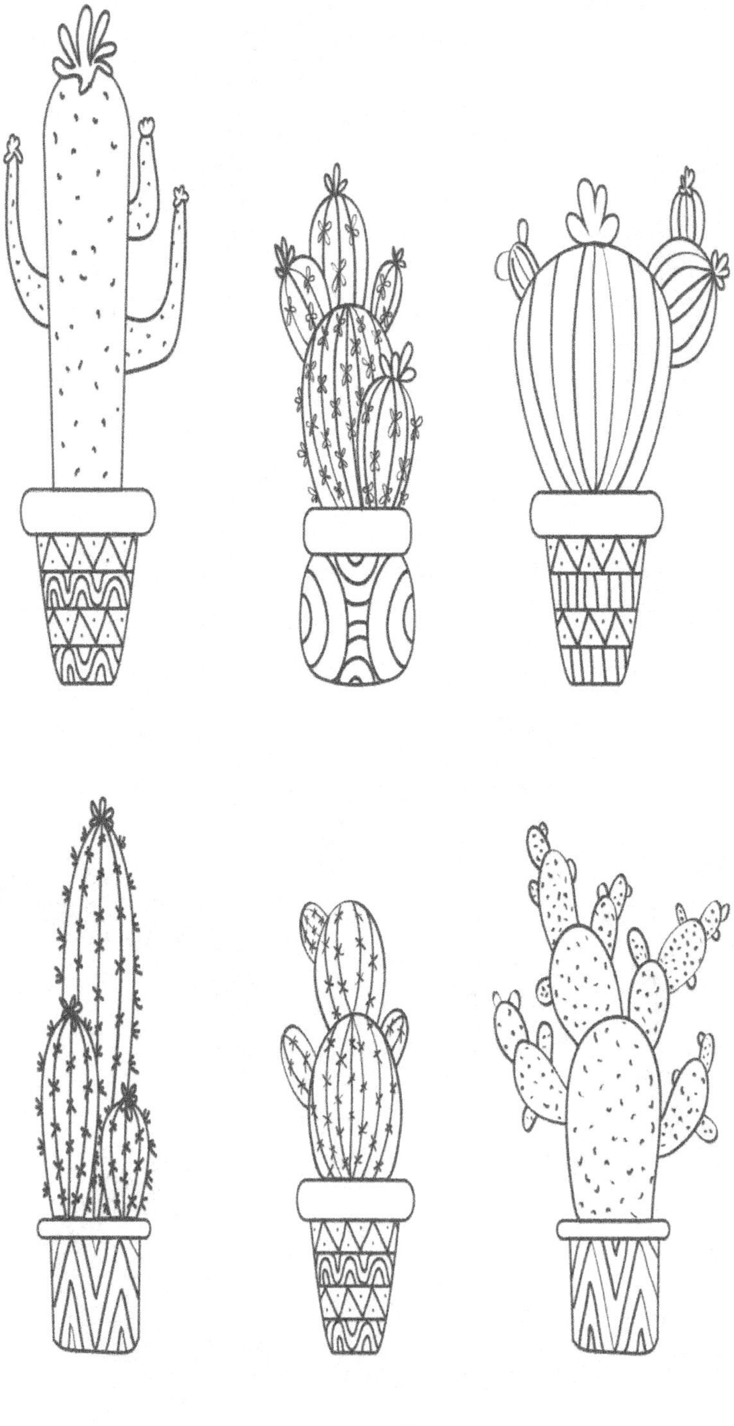

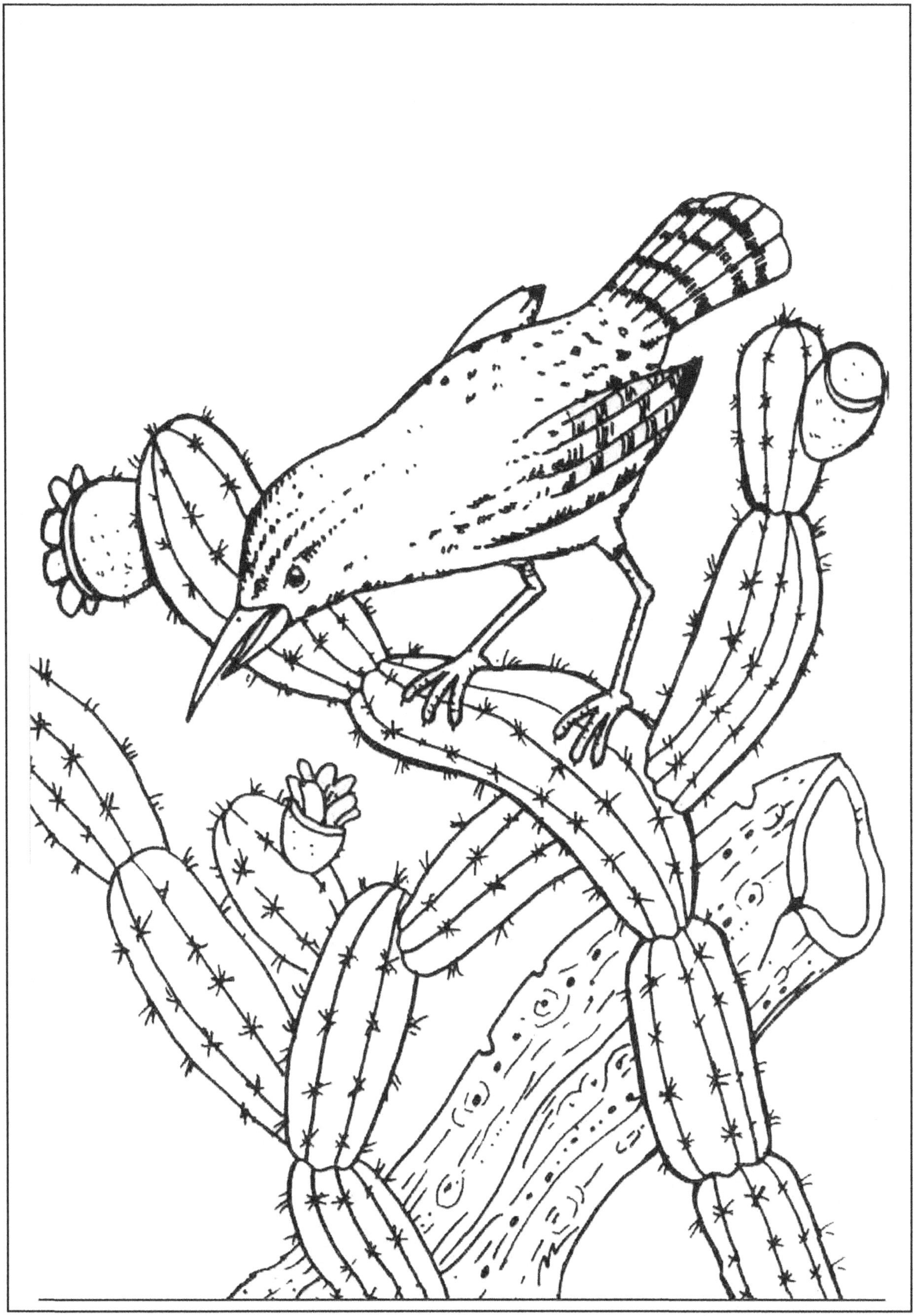

Valfré

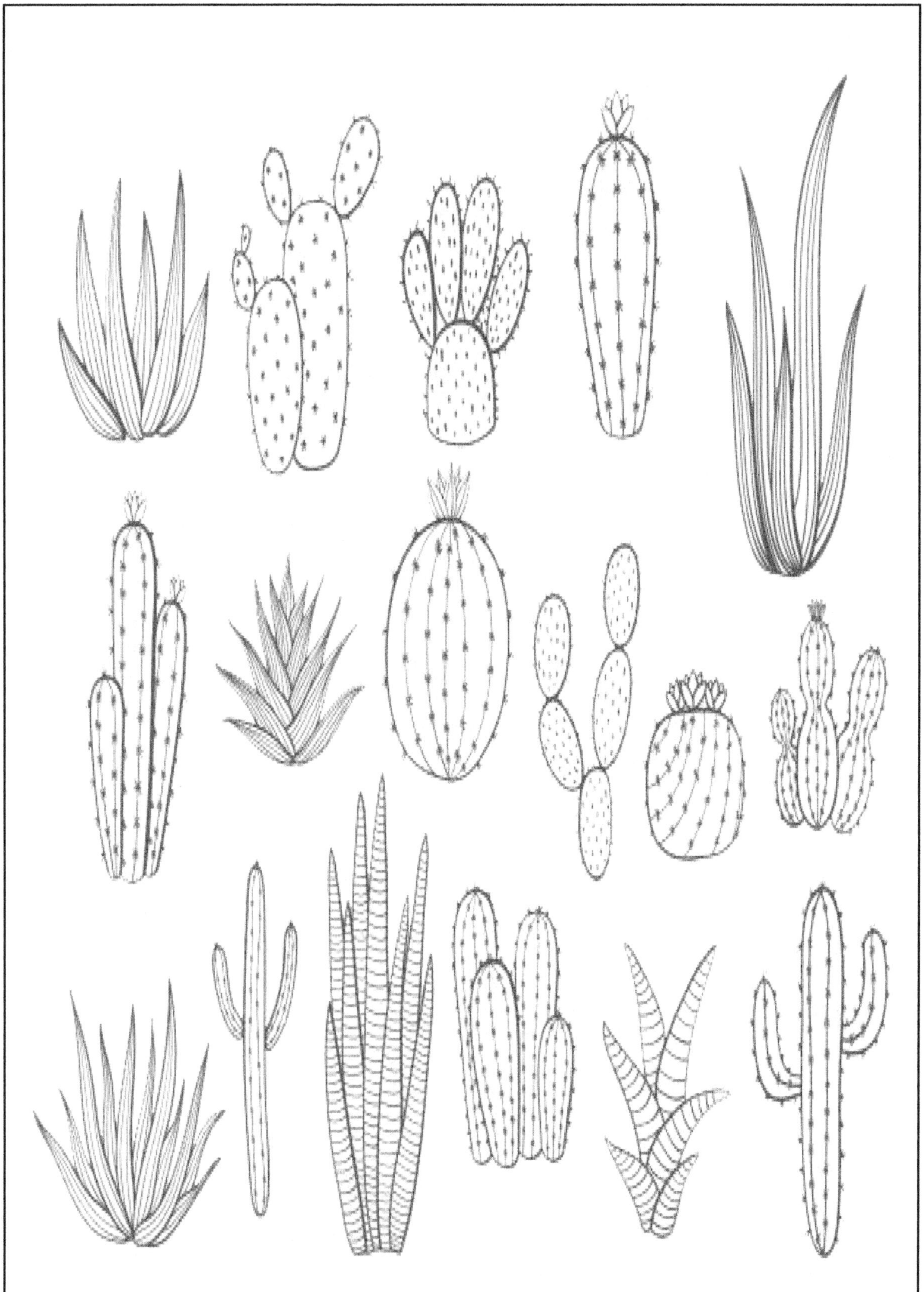

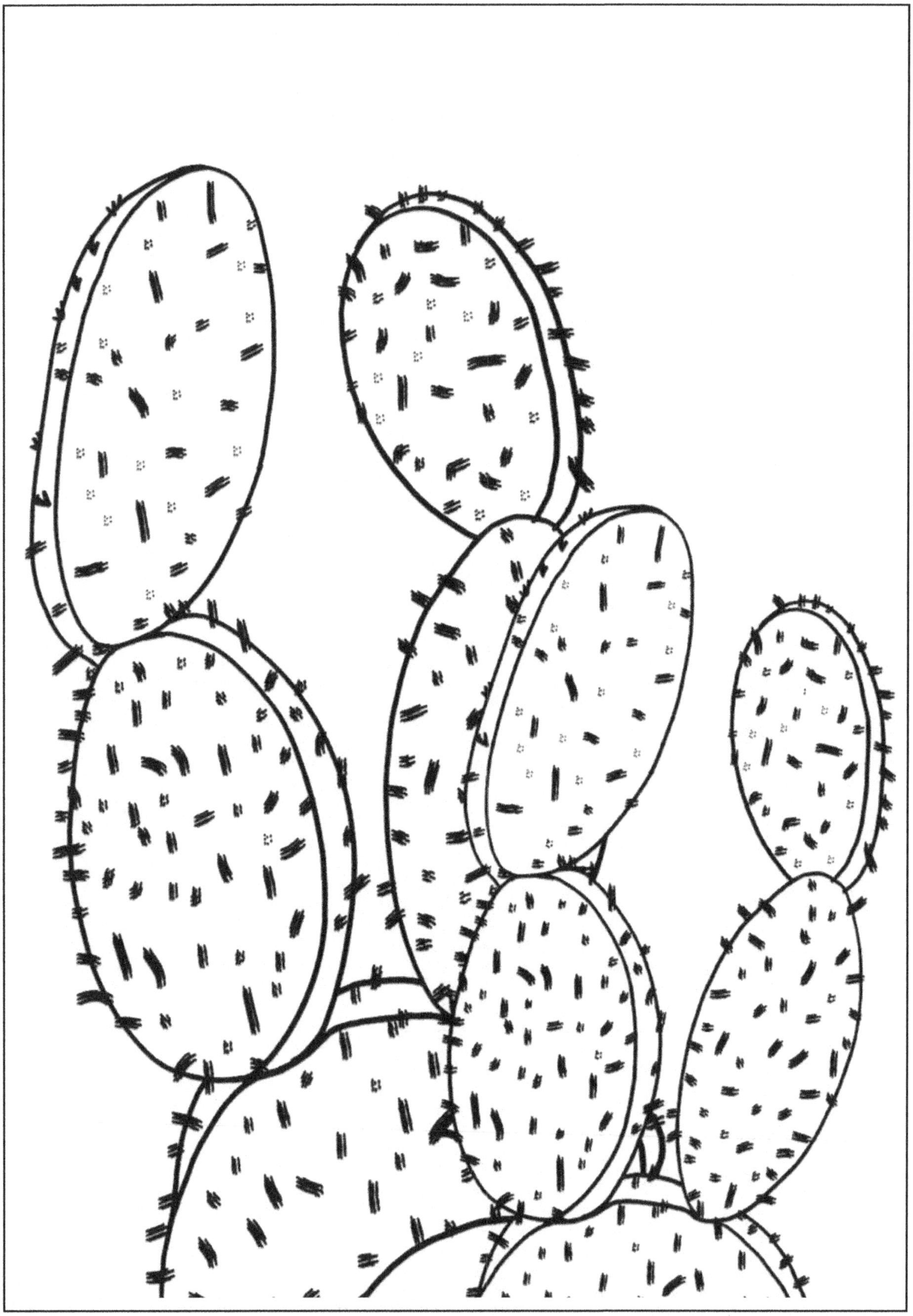

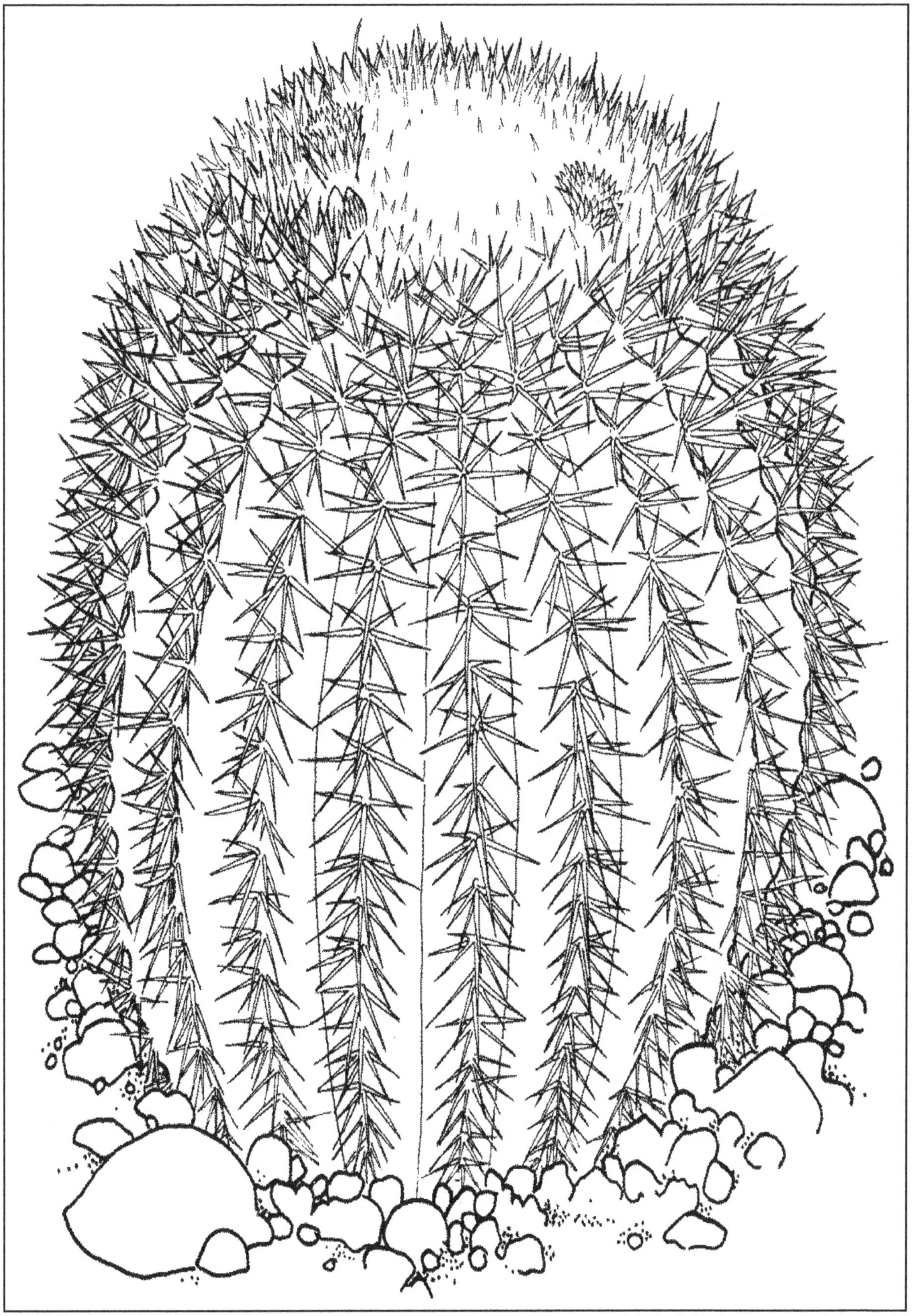

Cactus

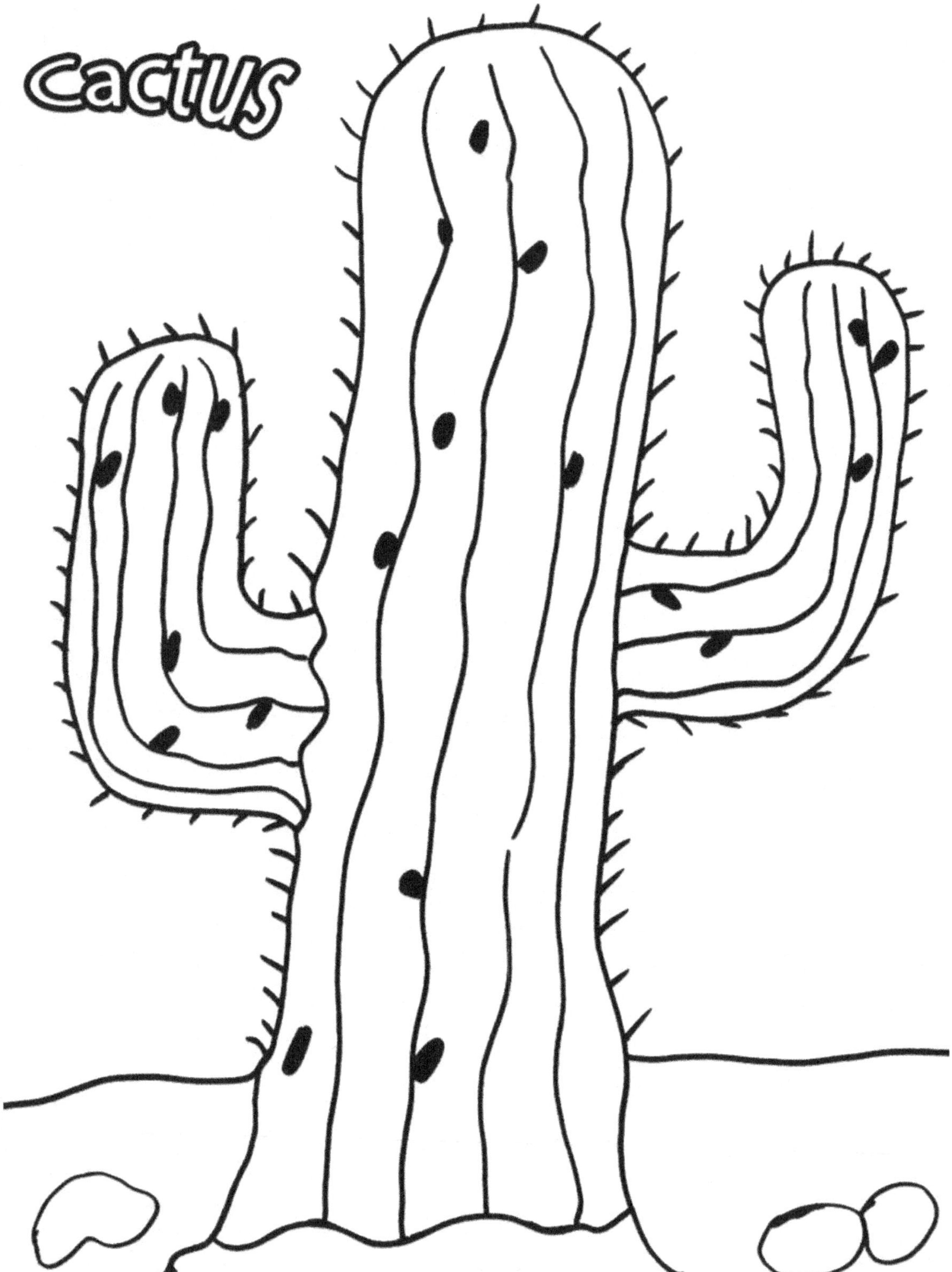

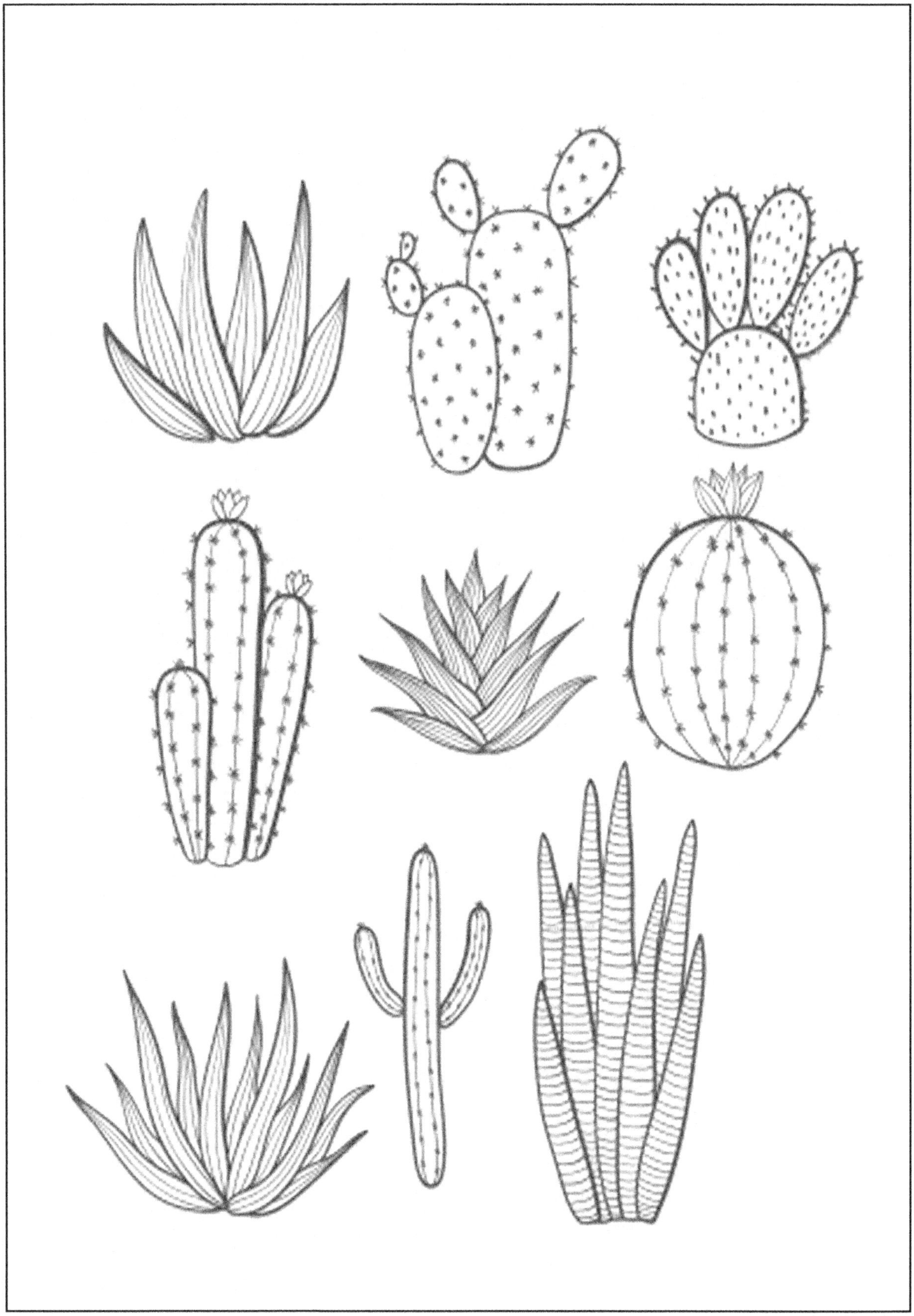

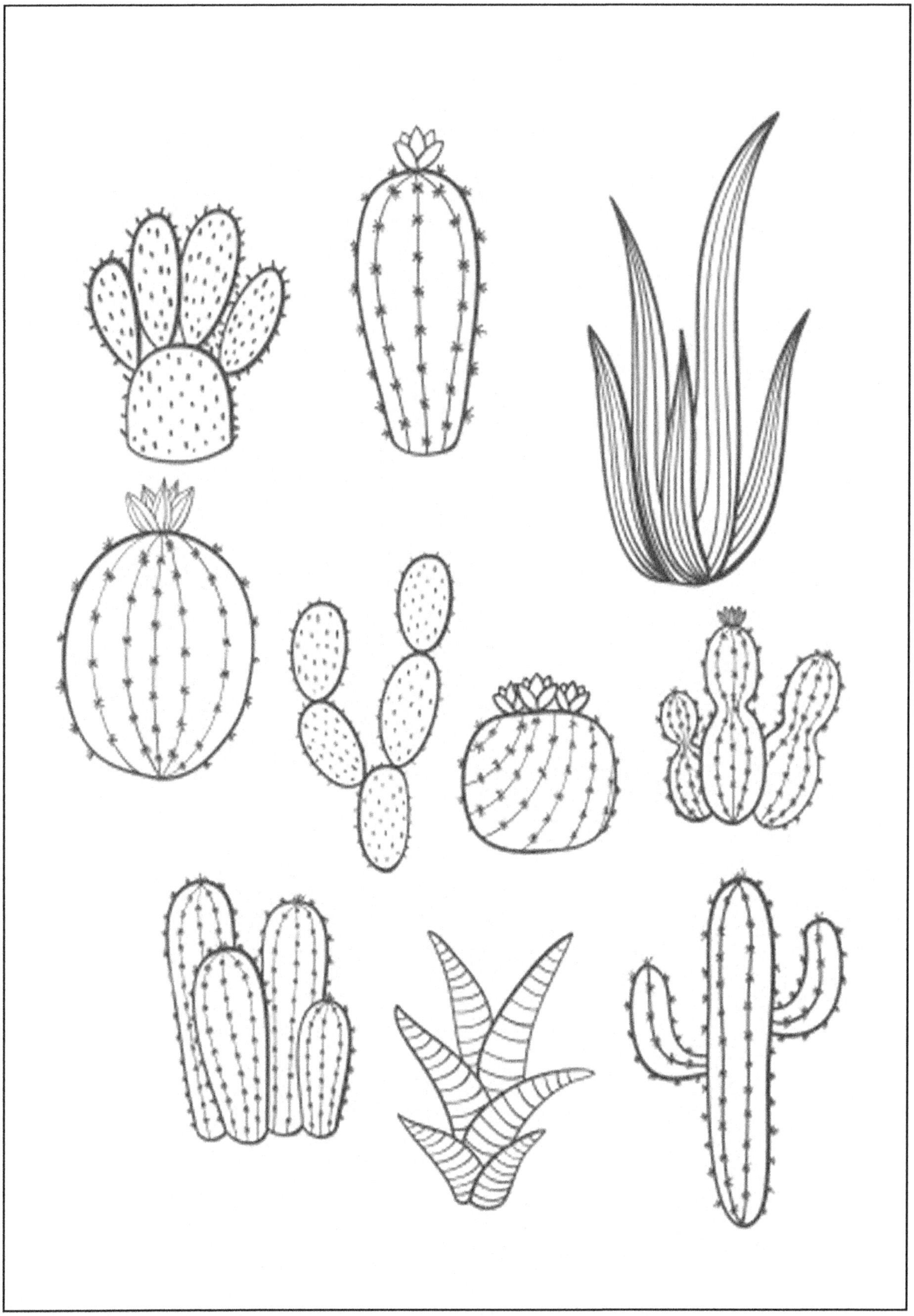

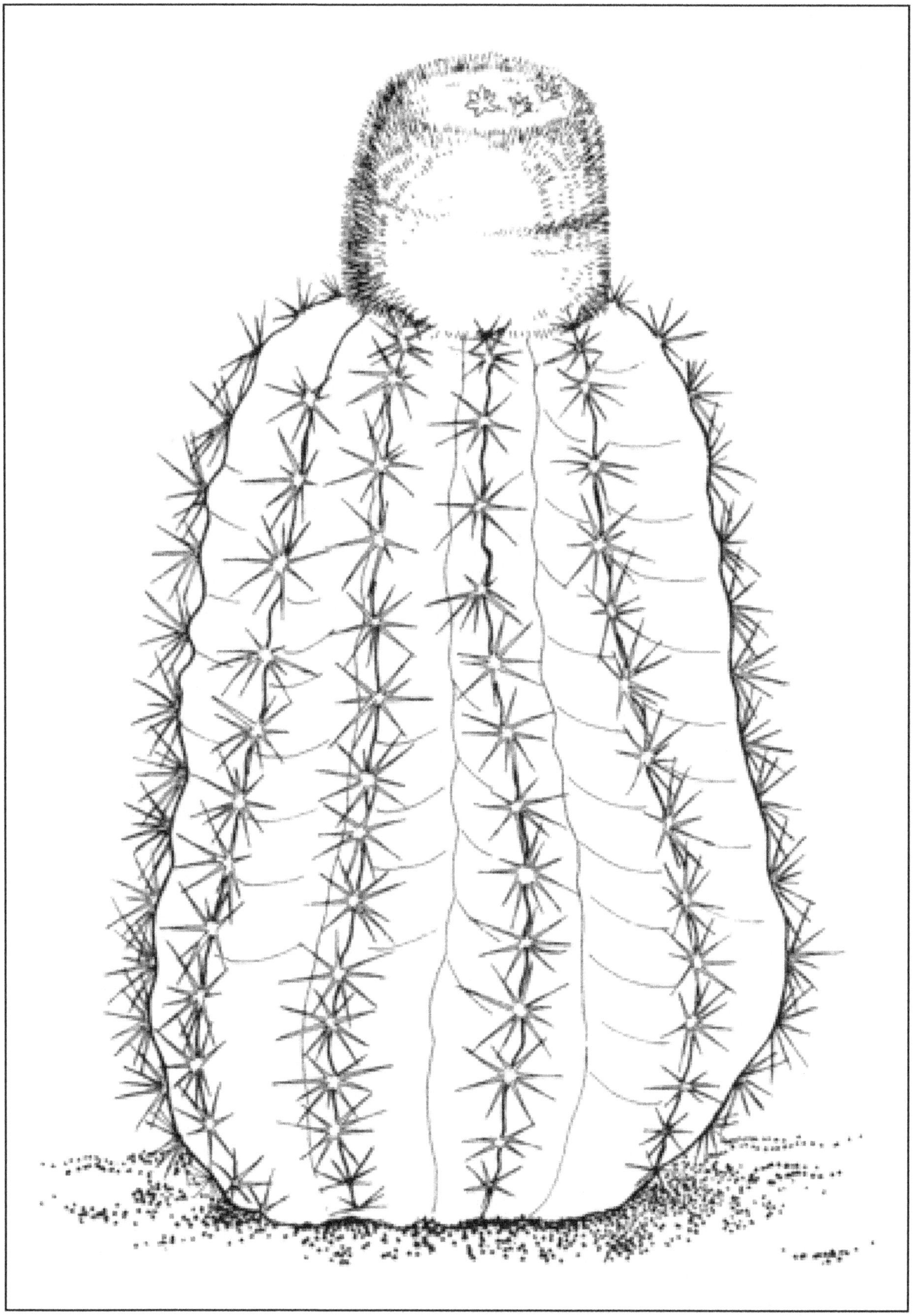

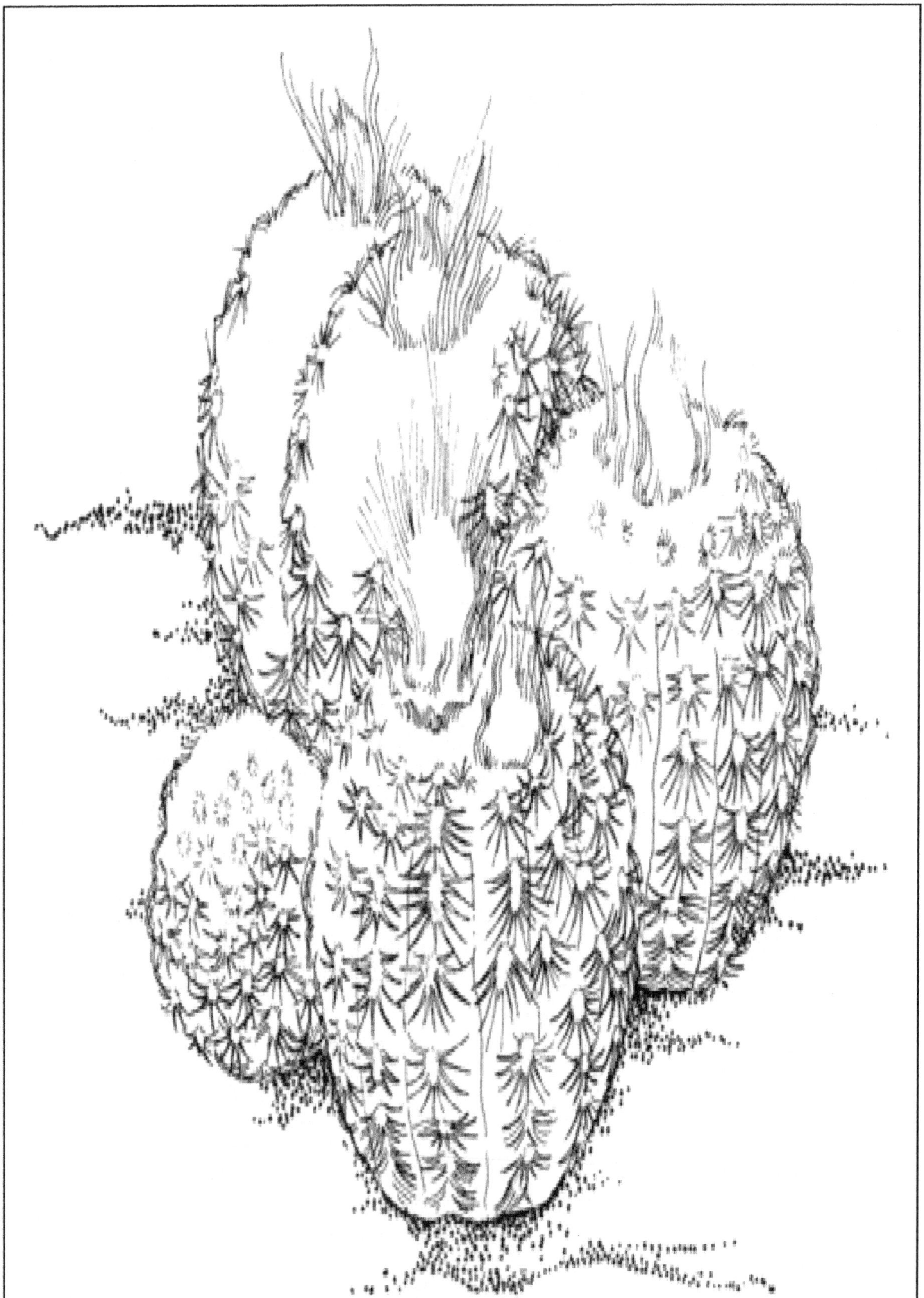

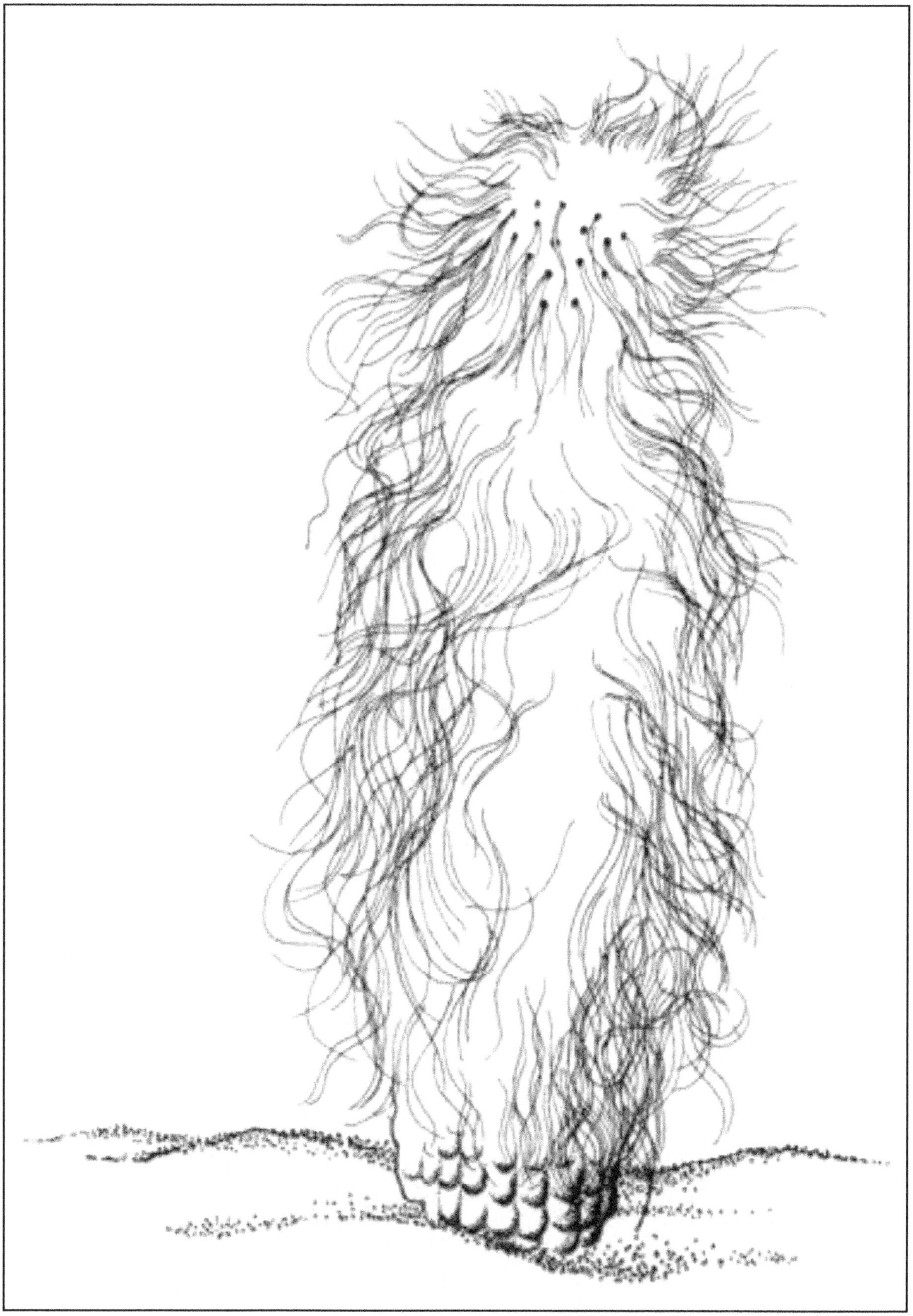

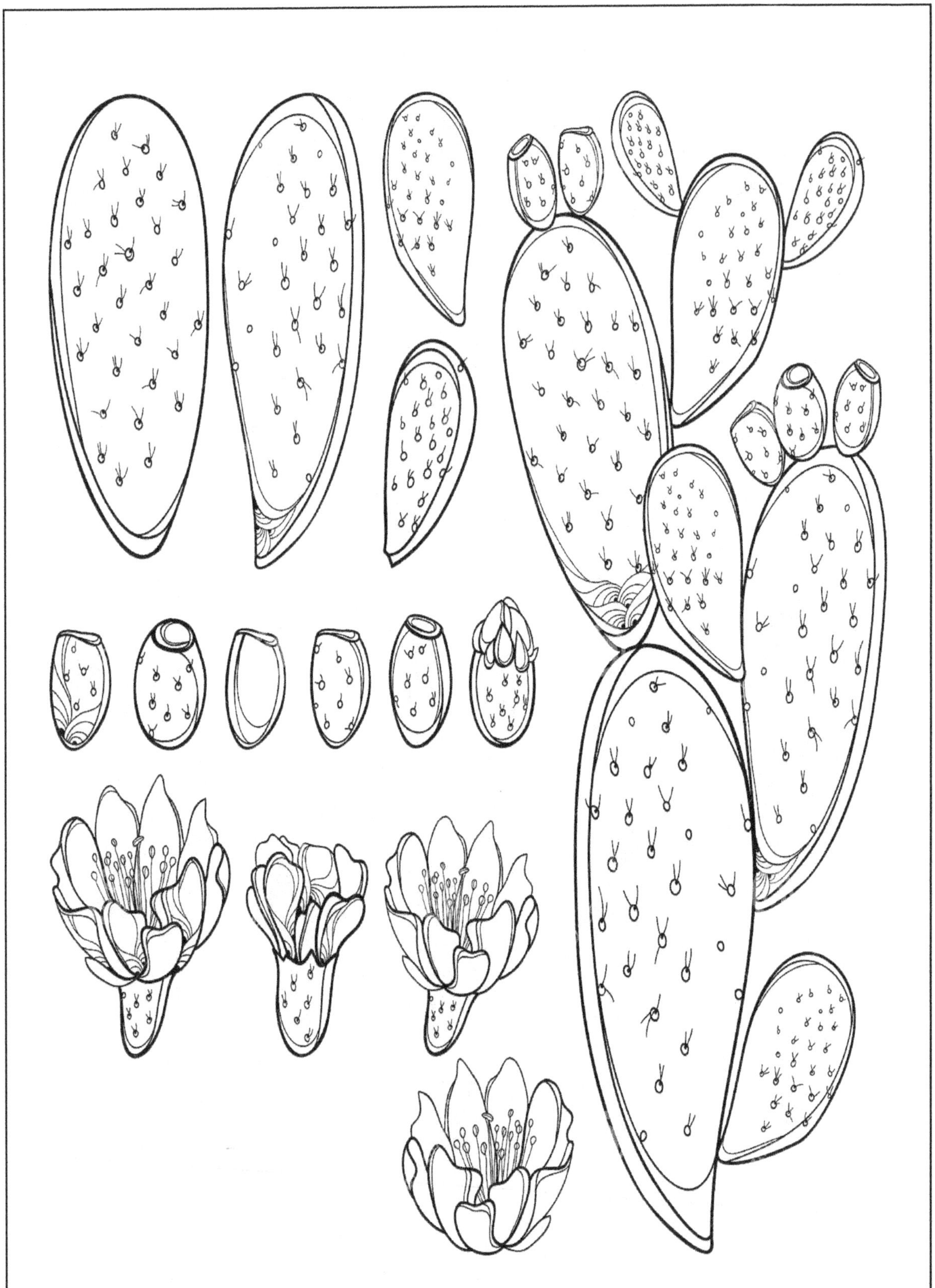

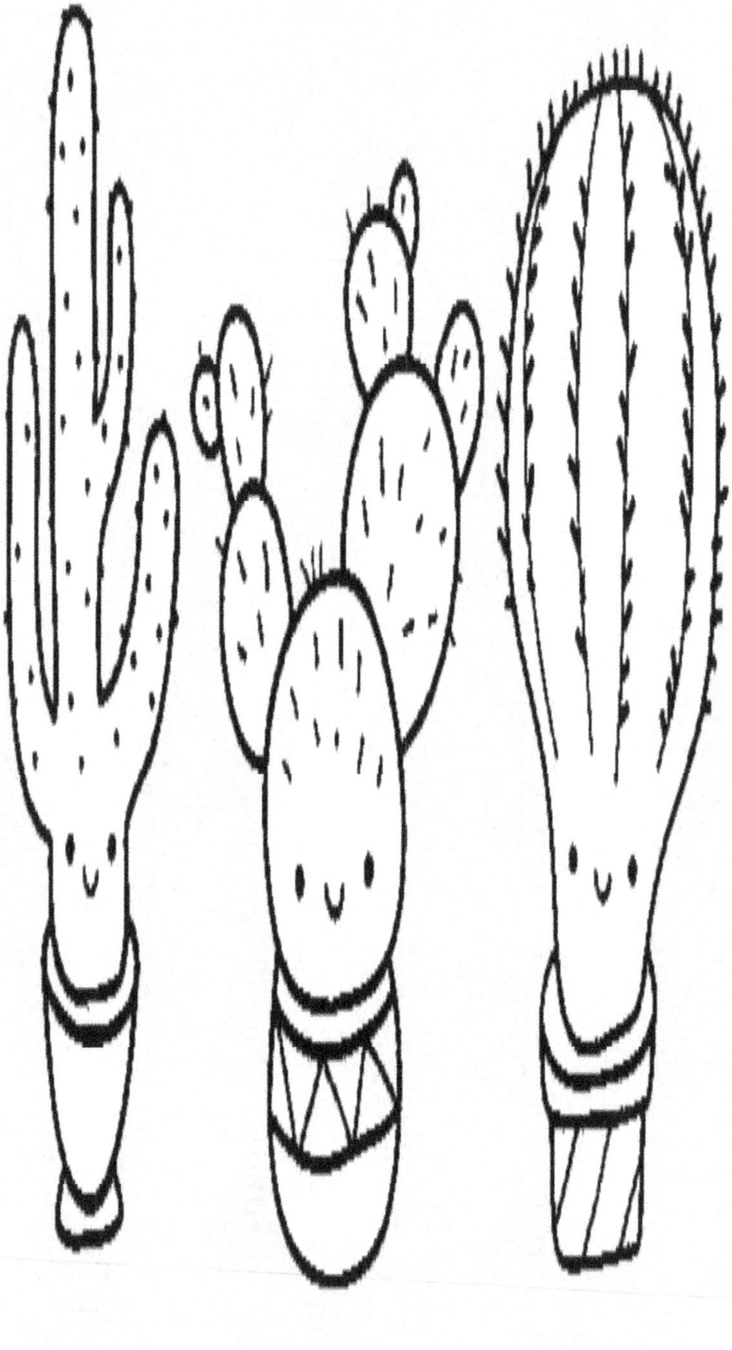

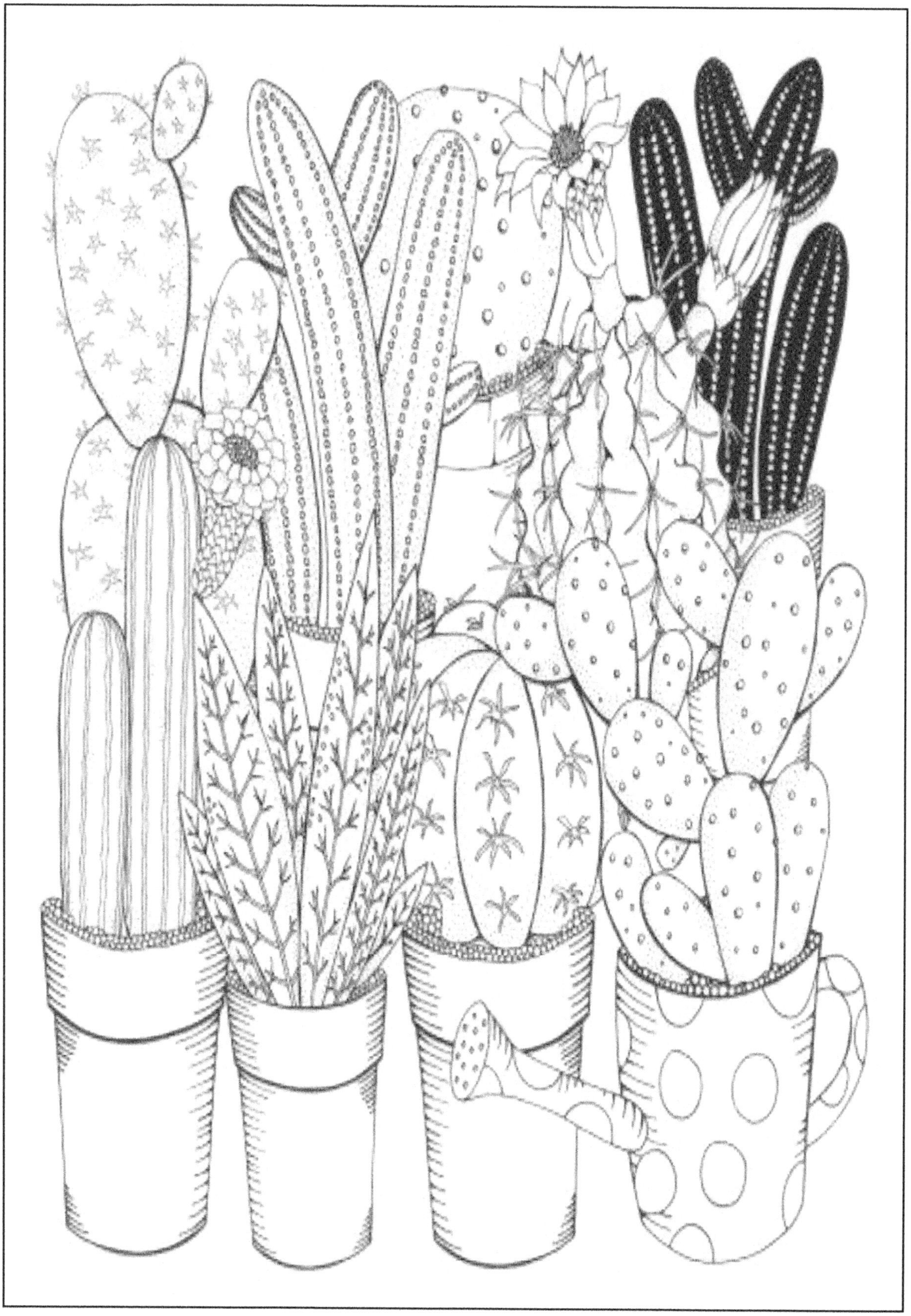

Made in the USA
Monee, IL
06 March 2021

62100821R00063